The Definitive Guide to E-commerce

KARLO PARKER

Copyright © 2023 Karlo Parker

All rights reserved.
ISBN: **9798399719740**

DEDICATION

This book is dedicated to the memory of my mother, who always supported me in everything I did and was a great inspiration to me. She was a wonderful person, full of love, wisdom, and patience, and she was always there for me in good times and bad.

Although she is no longer physically with me, her spirit always guides me and gives me strength to move forward. I am grateful to life for giving me the opportunity to have her as a mother, mentor, and friend, and I hope this book honors her memory and serves as a testament to my love and gratitude for her.

Mom, you will always be in my heart and mind, and I will carry you with me wherever I go. Thank you for everything you did for me and for being a constant source of love and support. I love you and miss you deeply.

INDEX

	DECICATION	i
1	Introduction to E-commerce	1
2	Creating an Online Store: Basic Steps	4
3	Selecting the Right Software for Your Online Store	7
4	Design and Development of the Online Store: Best Practices	11
5	Payment and Shipping Methods Configuration	15
6	Managing the Daily Operations of Your Online Store	20
7	Online Marketing Strategies for E-commerce	24
8	How to Optimize SEO for Your Online Store	29
9	Online Advertising: Effective Campaigns on Google and Facebook	33
10	Content Marketing: How to Attract and Retain Customers	39
11	Influencer Marketing: How to Use Influencers to Promote Your Online Store	43
12	Email Marketing: How to Build and Utilize an Effective Email List	48
13	Social Media Marketing: How to Utilize Social Media to Boost Sales	54
14	Measuring the Success of Your Online Marketing Strategy	59
15	Best Practices for Online Customer Service	63
16	How to Maintain a Base of Loyal and Satisfied Customers	68
17	How to Expand Your Business Internationally - A Guide to Global E-commerce	72

18 **Trends and Predictions for the Future of E-commerce**   76

ACKNOWLEDGEMENTS

I would like to take this opportunity to express my gratitude to all the people who have been an important part of the creation of this book. First and foremost, I want to thank my current partner, who has been a constant source of support, love, and motivation. Thank you for believing in me and encouraging me every step of the way.

I also want to thank my father, who has always supported me in everything I do. Your words of encouragement, advice, and presence in my life have been invaluable to me.
To my sisters, thank you for always being there in my life, your advice, and being my source of motivation during difficult times. Lastly, I want to express my gratitude to my children, who are my greatest inspiration and motivation in life.
 Thank you for teaching me the value of patience, perseverance, and unconditional love.

Without the support of these individuals, this book would not have been possible. I am grateful for their presence in my life and for everything they have done for me. Thank you from the bottom of my heart.

Chapter 1: Introduction to E-commerce

Currently, e-commerce has become one of the most popular ways of buying and selling goods and services.

Thanks to the increasing penetration of the Internet and mobile devices worldwide, e-commerce has experienced exponential growth in recent years. In fact, according to eMarketer estimates, global e-commerce will reach $5.8 trillion in 2022.

This growth is largely due to the convenience that e-commerce offers to consumers. The ability to buy any product from anywhere and at any time, and have it delivered to your doorstep, has transformed the way people shop.

Furthermore, e-commerce also presents a great opportunity for businesses. With an online store, businesses can reach a global audience, provide a personalized shopping experience, and significantly increase their revenue.

For example, a fashion company like ASOS, with an online store that offers free shipping and easy returns, has achieved great success. In 2020, ASOS reported a 23% increase in their online revenue compared to the previous year.

The Definitive Guide to E-commerce

Another company that has successfully leveraged the power of e-commerce is Amazon. With a wide selection of products, competitive prices, and fast shipping, Amazon has become one of the global e-commerce giants. However, e-commerce can also be a challenging landscape to navigate for those who are just starting out. From creating an online store to implementing an effective marketing strategy, the process can be demanding and require a lot of work.

That's why we have created "The Definitive Guide to E-commerce." In this guide, you will find a step-by-step approach to building a successful online store, as well as a guide to implementing an effective marketing strategy for your online store.

Throughout the book, we will show you how to create an attractive and user-friendly online store, how to select the right e-commerce software for your needs, and how to develop an effective marketing strategy to drive online sales.

Welcome to the world of e-commerce! We hope this guide serves as a valuable source of information and helps you succeed in your online business.

Chapter 2: Creating an Online Store: Basic Steps

Creating an online store is an exciting yet challenging process. There are many aspects to consider, from selecting a domain name to setting up the right e-commerce platform. In this chapter, we will guide you through the basic steps you need to follow to create your online store.

Step 1: Selecting a Domain Name and Web Hosting
The first step in creating an online store is to select a domain name and web hosting. The domain name is the web address of your online store, and web hosting is the online space where your store will be stored. Both are essential for your online store to function properly.

It's important to choose a domain name that is easy to remember and related to your brand or business. For example, the domain name "www.shoes.com" is easy to remember and clearly related to an online shoe store. Additionally, make sure to choose reliable and secure web hosting to ensure that your website is available to customers 24/7.

Step 2: Selecting an E-commerce Platform
Once you have selected a domain name and web hosting, it's time to choose an e-commerce platform. The e-commerce platform is the software that will allow you to create, customize, and manage your online store.

There are many options available, such as Shopify, WooCommerce, Magento, and many more. Each platform has its own features, benefits, and limitations. It's

The Definitive Guide to E-commerce

important to research and compare different options before making a decision.

Step 3: Designing and Developing the Online Store

After selecting the right e-commerce platform, it's time to design and develop your online store. It's important for the store to be attractive and user-friendly for customers.

Additionally, ensure that your online store has a frequently asked questions section and a clear return policy for customers.

In recent years, many companies have opted for minimalist and simple web designs that highlight products and services instead of cluttering the page with excessive information and visual content. Some examples of online stores with minimalist and effective designs are Apple, Everlane, and Allbirds.

Step 4: Setting Up Payment and Shipping Methods

After designing and developing the online store, it's time to set up payment and shipping methods. It's important to offer a variety of payment and shipping options so that customers can choose the one that best suits their needs.

Some popular payment options include PayPal, credit and debit cards, and bank transfers. As for shipping methods, you should consider factors such as shipping speed, cost, and delivery zone.

Step 5: Launching and Promoting the Online Store

After setting up payment and shipping methods, it's time to launch and promote your online store. It's important to note that launching the online store doesn't mean the work is done, but rather, it's just the beginning.

An effective marketing strategy is essential to drive online traffic and sales. Some of the most effective online marketing strategies include social media marketing, email marketing, online advertising, and content marketing.

It's important to keep in mind that an effective marketing strategy requires time and effort, but it can have a significant impact on the success of your online store.

Chapter 3: Selecting the Right Software for Your Online Store

In today's world, technology is essential to maintain competitiveness in e-commerce, and choosing the right software for your online store is crucial to its success. Make no mistake, this is a critical task that requires rigorous and detailed analysis.

To begin, it's important to define your goals and needs. Are you looking for open-source software or a commercial solution? How customizable should it be? What features are absolutely necessary? Once you have a clear idea of what you need, you can start exploring options that best suit your business.

But don't be swayed by the first solution you come across. Research, analyze, and compare the different available options. Pay attention to each software's features, scalability, and security, as well as ease of use and technical support.

When considering the cost of the software and the expected return on investment, it's important to keep in mind that the most expensive software isn't always the best, but you also don't want to skimp on a low-quality solution. Investing in software should be seen as an investment in the health and success of your business.

Lastly, ensure that the chosen software seamlessly integrates with your online store and payment platform.

Poor integration can lead to technical issues and loss of sales. Additionally, verify if the software offers customization options to fit the specific needs of your business.

Keep in mind that choosing the software for your online store is not something to be taken lightly. This is a crucial step that can make a difference between the triumph and failure of your online business. If chosen wisely, you will have the necessary technology to drive your business toward success.

According to a recent study by Statista, the global e-commerce market is expected to reach $6.5 trillion in 2023. This figure clearly shows the importance and potential for success of e-commerce worldwide.

Furthermore, it has been demonstrated that customers who have a good online shopping experience are more likely to return and make future purchases, leading to sustainable long-term growth for online businesses.
Therefore, choosing the right software for your online store is not only a matter of efficiency and effectiveness but also has a significant impact on customer satisfaction and, therefore, the success of your business. Invest in the right software, and you will see your online business thrive.

Creating your own online store has never been easier thanks to the wide variety of software options available in the market. To help you choose the best option, I present you with a list of the most popular and effective solutions.

Keep in mind that the choice of the right software will depend on your specific needs and goals, so I recommend researching and comparing before making a decision. However, the following options are a good starting point:

WooCommerce: It is one of the most widely used plugins for creating online stores on WordPress. This open-source software offers a wide range of customization options, allowing you to tailor the online store to the specific needs of your business.

Shopify: A commercial solution that offers a complete platform for creating and managing an online store. With a plethora of tools and customization options, Shopify is a popular choice for businesses seeking a comprehensive and user-friendly solution.

Magento: An open-source software that offers a wealth of advanced features for creating and managing an online store. Magento is a popular choice for businesses seeking a scalable and customizable solution.

BigCommerce: Another popular option in the commercial solutions market. With a wide variety of tools and customization options, BigCommerce is a popular choice for businesses seeking a comprehensive and user-friendly solution.

PrestaShop: An open-source software that offers a wide range of customization options and a user-friendly interface. PrestaShop is a popular choice for businesses seeking an easy-to-use and scalable solution.

OpenCart: An open-source software that offers a wide range of features and customization options. OpenCart is a popular choice for businesses seeking a low-cost and user-friendly solution.

With these software options, you'll be able to create and manage an online store that caters to your business needs and attracts a broad audience of potential customers.

So don't hesitate any longer, choose the right software and start building your online store today.

The Definitive Guide to E-commerce

Chapter 4: Design and Development of the Online Store: Best Practices

The design and development of your online store are crucial for the success of your online business. The aesthetics, functionality, and user-friendliness of your online store are critical factors that will determine your customers' shopping experience. Here are some of the best practices for designing and developing your online store.

First and foremost, the design of your online store should be attractive and consistent with your brand's image. The colors, fonts, and style should reflect your business's personality and values. The design should be visually appealing and easy to navigate, allowing your customers to find what they're looking for with ease.

Additionally, functionality and user-friendliness are key factors in the design and development of your online store. The navigation should be intuitive and easy to use, and the products should be organized into logical categories. It's important that customers can easily find what they're looking for, and that the checkout process is quick and straightforward.

A recent example of the importance of online store design and development can be found in the world of online fashion. The popular fashion brand Zara has invested significantly in improving its website and the shopping experience for its customers.

Zara has implemented a series of enhancements to its online store, including improving navigation and store structure, optimizing for mobile devices, and integrating new payment options. The brand has also improved the aesthetics of its online store by using high-quality images and an attractive and easy-to-navigate design.

As a result of these improvements, Zara has seen an increase in online sales and higher customer satisfaction. Customers have praised the user-friendliness and efficiency of Zara's online store, leading to increased loyalty and customer retention.

This example demonstrates how investing in the design and development of an online store can have a significant impact on success and customer satisfaction. Improvements in aesthetics,

functionality, and user-friendliness can lead to increased sales and higher customer retention. Therefore, it's essential for online businesses to pay attention to these critical factors and make the necessary investments to provide an optimal shopping experience for their customers.

Mobile optimization is another key factor in the design and development of your online store. More and more customers are making their online purchases from mobile devices, so it's crucial that your online store adapts to screens of all sizes. The online store should be easy to navigate on mobile devices, and buttons and links should be easy to press on touchscreens.

According to a recent survey, the use of mobile devices for online shopping continues to grow steadily. In 2021, it's estimated that 72% of online purchases worldwide will be made through mobile devices, representing a significant increase from 67% in 2019.

This statistic clearly illustrates the importance of mobile screen optimization in the online store. With over two-thirds of online purchases made through mobile devices, it's essential for online businesses to focus on optimizing their website to ensure an optimal shopping experience for their customers.

The lack of mobile screen optimization can lead to a decrease in conversion rates and lower customer satisfaction, negatively impacting the profitability and long-term success of the online business.
Regarding the development of your online store, it's crucial to choose a secure and stable programming language. Security is a critical factor in e-commerce, and it's essential for your online store to be secure and trustworthy.

Ensure that you use secure and reliable payment solutions and that your customers feel safe when entering their personal information.

Lastly, it's essential to conduct rigorous testing on your online store before launching it to the public. Make sure that all links work correctly, that products can be added to the cart, and that payments are processed smoothly. Testing is also an opportunity to identify and fix any errors or issues in your online store before they affect your customers' experience.

The design and development of your online store are key factors in attracting and retaining customers. Ensure that the design is attractive and consistent with your brand's image, and that the navigation is intuitive and user-friendly.

Mobile optimization is essential, and you must ensure that

your online store is secure and reliable. Conduct thorough testing to ensure that your online store is ready for the public and provides an optimal shopping experience for your customers. With careful design and development, you can drive the success of your online business.

Chapter 5: Payment and Shipping Methods Configuration

The success of an online store largely depends on the ease and security with which customers can make payments and receive their purchases. In this regard, proper configuration of payment and shipping methods is crucial to ensure an optimal shopping experience for customers.

In this chapter, we will address best practices for configuring payment and shipping methods in an online store. Firstly, it is important to offer a wide variety of payment options, ranging from credit cards and debit cards to virtual wallets and mobile payments. By doing so, customers can choose the payment method that best suits their needs and preferences.

The security of online payments is a critical issue for any online business, and it is essential to ensure the protection of customers' personal data. In this regard, it is important to implement appropriate security measures to safeguard customer data during online transactions.

One of the most effective methods to ensure the security of online payments is data encryption. This involves encoding credit card information and other personal customer data during online transactions. Data encryption ensures that customer information remains inaccessible to malicious third parties.

Another important measure to ensure the security of online payments is transaction verification.

Transaction verification is a process used to confirm the authenticity of a transaction and ensure there is no fraud. This may include verifying the credit card security code, billing address, and other relevant data.

Additionally, it is important to comply with online security regulations and standards, such as the Payment Card Industry Data Security Standard (PCI DSS). PCI DSS is a set of requirements used to ensure the security of online payment data. These requirements include implementing physical and logical security measures, protecting customer data, and conducting regular audits.

In conclusion, the security of online payments is essential for any online business. By implementing appropriate security measures such as data encryption and transaction verification, and complying with online security regulations and standards like PCI DSS, the protection of customer data and fraud prevention can be ensured. This can increase customer confidence in the online store and improve long-term profitability.

Proper configuration of shipping methods is crucial to providing online customers with a satisfactory shopping experience and, ultimately, increasing long-term loyalty. By offering shipping options that cater to customers' needs and preferences, customer satisfaction can be improved, and sales opportunities can be increased.

Free shipping is one of the most popular shipping options as it can attract customers and boost sales, especially for large or recurring orders. However, it is important to consider shipping costs and ensure that profit margins remain viable.

Express shipping is another popular option that provides fast delivery within an accelerated timeframe. This option can be appealing to customers who need to receive their orders quickly and are willing to pay an additional cost for expedited service.

Store pickup is a shipping option that may be attractive to customers who want to save on shipping costs and collect their order from a nearby store. This option can be particularly useful for retailers with a strong physical presence, as it can increase store visits and additional sales opportunities.

Providing detailed information about delivery times and shipping costs on the checkout page, and offering the option to track shipments online, is crucial. Detailed information about delivery times and shipping costs can help customers make informed decisions and reduce friction during the checkout process.

Furthermore, the option to track shipments online can increase customer confidence and alleviate concerns about delivery. By providing customers with a way to track their package in real-time, the shopping experience can be enhanced, and customer satisfaction can be increased.

A successful example of a company that has implemented an effective shipping and returns strategy is Zappos, owned by Amazon. Since 2003, the company has offered free shipping and an unrestricted time return policy, leading to increased customer satisfaction and loyalty. The company has demonstrated that offering shipping options that cater to customer needs is an effective way to differentiate from competitors and improve long-term profitability.

Remember that proper configuration of shipping methods is crucial to ensuring a satisfactory shopping experience for online customers. By offering shipping options that cater to customers' needs and preferences, providing detailed information about delivery times and shipping costs, and offering the option to track shipments online, customer satisfaction can be improved, and long-term profitability can be increased.

Chapter 6: Managing the Daily Operations of Your Online Store

Proper management of the daily operations of your online store is essential for the long-term success of your business. A company that has achieved excellent management of its daily operations is Warby Parker, an online retailer of eyewear and accessories.

Warby Parker has implemented a highly efficient inventory management system that allows them to track inventory in real-time and adjust stock levels based on customer demand. Additionally, the company has established a network of reliable suppliers and manufacturers to ensure that products are available to customers at all times.

The company has also emphasized the importance of excellent customer service in its daily operations. Warby Parker has implemented a customer support system focused on quickly and efficiently resolving issues, leading to high levels of customer satisfaction and long-term loyalty.

Returns management is a critical aspect of the daily operations of any online store, and Warby Parker has successfully implemented a hassle-free return policy that has significantly improved customer satisfaction. The company understands that customers may change their minds or simply not be satisfied with the received product, and therefore, they have established a policy that allows customers to return their products within a 30-day period without questions asked.

Warby Parker's hassle-free return policy focuses on providing a worry-free shopping experience for customers. Customers can return their products without having to justify their decision, which fosters customer trust and reduces friction during the return process. Additionally, the company ensures that the return process is easy and hassle-free for the customer.

Warby Parker's hassle-free return policy has had a significant impact on customer satisfaction and customer loyalty. Warby Parker customers report high levels of satisfaction, which has led to increased trust and customer loyalty. Furthermore, the hassle-free return policy has helped Warby Parker differentiate itself from competitors and increase long-term profitability.

It is important to remember that proper returns management can be a valuable tool for customer satisfaction and business profitability in the online world. By implementing a hassle-free return policy, providing an easy return process, and ensuring that customers are informed about return policies, customer satisfaction and loyalty can be significantly improved.

Payment management is a crucial aspect in e-commerce, and therefore, it is important to have a dedicated and trained team to ensure a secure and satisfactory payment experience for customers. The number of people required for this team will depend on the size and complexity of the online store, but at a minimum, a group of payment management specialists will be required.

The payment manager will oversee and coordinate all payment operations, ensuring that security standards and online regulations are met. The online security specialist, on the other hand, will be responsible for implementing and maintaining appropriate security measures to protect customer information and reduce the risk of fraud.

The data analyst will be responsible for monitoring and analyzing the flow of transactions to detect patterns and trends, allowing for improved payment strategy and predicting future needs. And finally, the customer experience specialist will ensure that the payment experience is easy, fast, and secure for the customer.

Each of these specialists will play an important role in online payment management. Together, they will ensure effective transaction management and the security of customer information. Payment management is a crucial aspect of e-commerce and, if done effectively, can significantly improve customer satisfaction and business profitability.

In summary, efficient management of daily operations is essential for the long-term success of any online business. Warby Parker is an example of how proper inventory management, order fulfillment, customer service, and returns management can improve efficiency and profitability of a company. By following best practices in managing daily operations, your online store can achieve long-term success and customer loyalty.

Chapter 7: Online Marketing Strategies for E-commerce

Online marketing is essential for the success of e-commerce. Just like any other business, an online store needs to be promoted to attract and retain customers. In this chapter, we will explore some of the most effective online marketing strategies for e-commerce.

One of the most effective strategies is online advertising, such as Google ads and social media ads. Online ads can be targeted to specific audiences based on location, interests, and other demographic criteria, making them highly effective in reaching potential customers.

An example of a company that has successfully used online advertising is the footwear and accessories brand, Toms. The company has used Google ads and social media ads to reach its target audience and increase sales.

Toms has used online advertising to promote its One for One initiative, where for every pair of shoes purchased, the company donates a pair to a person in need. The company has used ads targeted at people interested in corporate social responsibility and charitable causes, which has allowed them to effectively reach their target audience.

Toms' online advertising strategy has been highly effective and has helped the company increase its customer base and long-term profitability. The focus on corporate social responsibility and promotion of charitable causes has also helped the company differentiate itself from competitors and create a more appealing brand for consumers.

Another effective strategy is content marketing, which involves creating and distributing useful and relevant content to attract and retain customers. Content marketing can include blogs, infographics, videos, and other content formats that solve customer problems and provide valuable information.

Content marketing has proven to be a very effective strategy in e-commerce. According to HubSpot, companies that publish content on their blog are 434% more likely to be better ranked by search engines and therefore receive more organic traffic to their website. Additionally, 47% of consumers say they have seen three to five pieces of content before making an online purchase. These statistics demonstrate the importance of content marketing in e-commerce and its ability to attract and retain customers. Email marketing is another powerful online marketing tool for e-commerce. Email can be used to send promotions, offers, and product updates to existing and potential customers. It is important to personalize the email content to make it relevant and engaging for the recipients.

Email marketing is one of the most effective tools for online marketing in e-commerce. In fact, according to a DMA Insights report, email has an average return on investment of $42 for every dollar spent, making it one of the most cost-effective marketing tactics. This profitability is due to its ability to reach existing and potential customers directly and personalize content to make it relevant and engaging.

Furthermore, email is highly effective for retaining existing customers, with 80% of online retailers reporting it as their most effective marketing tool for customer retention. By sending promotions, offers, and product updates via email, customers can be kept interested in the brand and motivated to make additional purchases.

Another advantage of email is its ability to measure and analyze results. Retailers can measure email open rates, click-throughs, and conversions, allowing them to adjust their marketing strategy accordingly.
Lastly, influencer marketing can be an effective strategy for reaching specific audiences. Influencers are online influential individuals with a large following and can be hired to promote products and services to their audience.

A successful example of an online marketing strategy is the case of Fenty Beauty, a makeup brand owned by singer Rihanna. The brand was launched in 2017 with an aggressive digital marketing strategy, including online advertising, content marketing, and the use of fashion and beauty influencers to promote the brand.

Fenty Beauty used Instagram as its primary online marketing platform, creating an official account that showcased makeup products and their usage on different skin tones. The brand also collaborated with fashion and beauty influencers from diverse ethnicities and cultural backgrounds, helping them reach a diverse audience and expand their customer base.

Fenty Beauty's digital marketing strategy was highly effective, helping the brand achieve success in a short period of time. In just its first month of launch, the brand generated over $72 million in sales and received acclaim for its inclusivity and diversity.

In summary, online marketing is essential for the success of e-commerce. By utilizing effective strategies such as online advertising, content marketing, email marketing, and influencer marketing, online stores can reach specific audiences and increase sales. The successful case of Fenty

Beauty demonstrates how a well-planned and executed digital marketing strategy can lead to e-commerce success.

Chapter 8: How to Optimize SEO for Your Online Store

SEO optimization is essential for any online business looking to improve its visibility and attract traffic to its website. Thorough keyword research is the first step in optimizing your e-commerce website's SEO. By identifying relevant keywords for your niche and your customers' search needs, you can optimize your website's content to increase visibility in search engines.

However, keyword research alone is not enough; it is important to implement them properly on your website. It is crucial to ensure that these keywords are included in your site's content, page titles and subtitles, and product descriptions. Additionally, it is essential for your website's structure to be user-friendly and search engine-friendly, meaning that pages should be well-organized and linked coherently.

The most important factors in SEO optimization include:

- Thorough keyword research relevant to your niche and your customers' search needs.

- Optimization of your website's content, including titles, descriptions, header tags, and meta descriptions, to improve readability and relevance for search engines and customers.

- Optimization of your website's structure, ensuring that pages are well-organized and interlinked coherently.

- Website speed, which refers to the site's loading speed, is a critical factor in improving user experience and search engine ranking.

- Implementation of proper link-building practices to obtain high-quality and relevant backlinks to your website.

A study by HubSpot demonstrated that 75% of users never click beyond the first page of search results, highlighting the importance of appearing in the top search results to increase visibility and attract traffic to your website. Additionally, another study by Backlinko found that pages ranking in the first position of Google search results have an average click-through rate of 31.7%.

Optimizing your website's structure and content is crucial to ensure that your products and services are easily accessible to your potential customers. By optimizing titles, descriptions, header tags, and meta descriptions, you can improve your website's readability for search engines and attract the right customers to your site.

An example of optimizing the structure and content of an e-commerce website is Etsy, an online sales platform. On this website, product titles are clear and descriptive, and descriptions are detailed and well-organized. Additionally, header tags and meta descriptions are carefully crafted to be relevant and appealing to search engines and potential customers.

Through optimizing the structure and content of their website, Etsy has significantly improved their visibility in search engines and attracted a large number of potential customers to their site. Furthermore, by making their products easily accessible and readable, they have enhanced the user experience and conversion rate on their website.

Website speed is another important factor for SEO optimization. Slow-loading websites can negatively impact user experience and search engine rankings. According to a Google study, 53% of users abandon a website if it takes more than three seconds to load. Therefore, it is essential to optimize your website's speed by compressing images, using caching tools, and removing unnecessary elements on the site.

SEO optimization is fundamental to the success of any online store. Thorough keyword research, optimization of website structure and content, and website speed are critical factors in improving visibility and user experience. With good SEO optimization, you can increase website traffic, improve customer satisfaction, and boost sales for your online business.

Chapter 9: Online Advertising: Effective Campaigns on Google and Facebook

Nowadays, online advertising is one of the most powerful tools to attract potential customers to your online store. Google and Facebook are two of the most popular platforms for online advertising, with millions of active users worldwide. In this chapter, we will discuss how to create effective campaigns on Google and Facebook to boost traffic and sales for your online store.

Google Campaigns

Advertising on Google allows advertisers to reach a highly specific audience based on user search. According to a study by Wordstream, the average click-through rate for Google search ads is 3.17%, meaning that Google ads can be highly effective in reaching potential customers.

To create an effective campaign on Google, it is important to conduct keyword research and select the right keywords for your ad. Additionally, the quality and relevance of your website's content are crucial to the success of your Google ads, as Google evaluates the quality of your website when determining the positioning of your ad on the search results page.

There are many effective ways to run advertising campaigns on Google, but some of the most common ones include:

- Search ads: These ads appear in Google search results when someone searches for a relevant keyword related to your business. Search ads are highly effective because they allow you to reach people who are already looking for what you offer. For example, if you have an online shoe store, you can create search ads for keywords like "women's shoes" or "men's dress shoes."

- Display ads: Display ads are graphical ads that appear on other websites. These ads can include images, text, and videos and can be targeted to specific audiences based on their interests, browsing behavior, and geographic location. For example, if you sell baby clothing, you can create a display ad to appear on a popular maternity or parenting website.

- Remarketing ads: Remarketing ads allow you to reach people who have already visited your website. These ads will appear on other websites that those people visit after leaving your site. Remarketing ads are effective because they allow you to reach people who have already shown interest in your business. For example, if a user visited your website but didn't complete a purchase, you can show them a remarketing ad to remind them about your product or service.

According to Statista, in 2020, 86.6% of Google's advertising revenue came from search ads, while 13.4% came from display ads and other ad formats. These data highlight the effectiveness of search ads on Google in reaching potential customers.

Facebook Campaigns

Advertising on Facebook allows advertisers to reach a highly specific audience based on location, interests, and other demographic criteria. According to a study by Hootsuite, the average cost per click (CPC) on Facebook is $1.72, making it one of the most cost-effective advertising platforms.

To create an effective campaign on Facebook, it is important to have a clear and defined target audience. Facebook offers a variety of targeting tools to help you reach your target audience, including location, age, interests, and online behaviors. Additionally, the content of your Facebook ad should be engaging and relevant to your target audience to increase click-through rates and conversions.

There are various ways to run effective campaigns on Facebook, and the choice of strategy will depend on the specific goals of each online business. Here are some examples of advertising campaigns on Facebook:

1. Carousel ads: This option allows you to display multiple images or videos in a single ad, showcasing different products or features of a product in one ad. According to Facebook studies, carousel ads have 30-50% lower cost per conversion and 20-30% higher conversion rates compared to single-image ads.

2. Video ads: Video ads can be an effective way to capture and retain audience attention, and they have been shown to have higher conversion rates compared to other types of ads on Facebook. According to HubSpot studies, video ads on Facebook have an

average click-through rate of 4.20%, making them one of the most effective forms of online advertising.

3. Remarketing ads: This strategy involves showing specific ads to people who have already interacted with your website or online products. Remarketing ads have a high conversion potential as they target people who have already shown interest in your products or services. According to Google studies, remarketing ads can increase conversions by 161%.

4. Special offers ads: Special offers ads, such as discounts, promotions, and free shipping, can be an effective way to attract and convert potential customers on Facebook. According to Shopify studies, discounts are the most effective special offer for increasing online sales.

Statistics on Online Advertising

According to a study by eMarketer, worldwide spending on online advertising is expected to reach $605.08 billion in 2021.

According to a study by Wordstream, 41% of clicks on Google ads occur in the top three search results.

According to a study by Hootsuite, 93% of social media marketers use Facebook for online advertising.
According to a study by Facebook, video ads on Facebook have a 20% higher conversion rate than image ads.

In summary, online advertising can be a highly effective tool to boost traffic and sales for your online store. Keyword research and content quality are key to the success of Google ads, while audience targeting and content relevance are crucial for Facebook ads. With proper optimization and continuous measurement of your advertising campaign's performance, you can significantly increase traffic and sales for your online store.

Chapter 10: Content Marketing: How to Attract and Retain Customers

In an increasingly competitive online market, brands must find ways to stand out and connect with their customers in an authentic and meaningful way. Content marketing has become an essential strategy to achieve this, allowing brands to create and share valuable and relevant content that addresses the problems and needs of their customers.

Unlike traditional marketing, which focuses on selling products, content marketing is centered around building lasting relationships through customer trust and loyalty. By providing useful and high-quality information, brands can establish themselves as leaders in their field and improve customers' perception of them.

Furthermore, content marketing not only enhances the relationship between the brand and the customer, but it can also improve search engine rankings and increase website traffic. By creating SEO-optimized content, brands can attract new customers and foster long-term loyalty.

Another example of effective content marketing is through the creation of informative and entertaining videos. Videos can be a powerful tool to convey information about a product or service in an engaging manner and also help create an emotional connection with the customer.

Content marketing has evolved to adapt to changes in how customers consume information and content online. Videos have become a valuable tool for brands seeking to effectively and attractively convey information to their potential customers. Customers prefer watching a video about a product or service rather than reading about it, which means videos are an essential tool for conveying information and establishing an emotional connection with customers. Brand videos also have a high level of attention retention, meaning that customers engage with and remember the information presented in the video for longer than other content formats.

A great example of a successful content marketing campaign is Blendtec's "Will it Blend?" video series. The campaign used entertaining and unique videos to showcase the blending capabilities of their blenders, generating significant online attention and excitement. The campaign quickly spread on social media and was widely shared online, helping increase the brand's visibility and attract new customers. As a result, Blendtec's sales increased by 700%, demonstrating the effectiveness of content marketing in driving online business growth.

Another example of a successful content marketing campaign is John Deere's "The Furrow" blog and video series. John Deere, an agricultural machinery company, presents stories and tips related to farming and rural life, which helps build a community of loyal followers and attract new customers to the brand. The campaign has helped establish John Deere as an authority in the agricultural industry and increase long-term customer loyalty.

Glossier, a cosmetics brand, is another example of an effective content marketing strategy. The brand has built a large base of followers and loyal customers through its focus on attractive and useful content. Glossier has created an active online community with a blog full of beauty and lifestyle content, as well as an active presence on social media. The brand has also launched popular products based on customer feedback, helping foster customer loyalty and satisfaction.

In summary, content marketing is a powerful tool for attracting and retaining customers in e-commerce. Whether through a well-managed blog, informative and entertaining videos, or an effective social media strategy, brands can create meaningful connections with their customers and increase long-term sales.

Chapter 11: Influencer Marketing: How to Use Influencers to Promote Your Online Store

Influencer marketing has become a popular tool for brands looking to promote their products or services online. Influencers are individuals with a large following on social media and can help brands reach a broader audience and attract new customers. In this chapter, we will explore how to effectively utilize influencers to promote your online store and enhance your marketing outcomes.

Firstly, it is important to identify the right influencers for your brand. Not all influencers are suitable for every brand, so you need to carefully research and find those that align with your niche and marketing goals. Factors to consider include the number of followers, the quality of their content, their audience demographics, and their style to ensure they are a good fit for your brand.

To identify the appropriate influencers for your brand, you can utilize various tools and platforms. A popular option is to use influencer search tools such as BuzzSumo or Hootsuite Insights, which allow you to search by keywords and filter by audience size, location, and other important factors. You can also leverage influencer marketing platforms like AspireIQ, Upfluence, or HYPR, which enable you to connect with influencers and manage collaborations more efficiently. Additionally, social media platforms like Instagram and YouTube have built-in tools that allow you to search for and connect with relevant influencers in your niche. By utilizing these tools, you can find the right influencers for your brand and maximize the return on investment for your influencer marketing campaigns.

Once you have identified the appropriate influencers, it is important to establish a relationship with them. You can reach out to them directly through their social media channels or via email and offer them a collaboration where they promote your products or services in exchange for compensation or benefits. It is important to set clear expectations and ensure that both parties understand the terms of the collaboration.

In the current era of influencer marketing, authenticity is key. Consumers increasingly value honesty and transparency, and they expect brands to be transparent about their collaborations with influencers. To ensure authenticity in your influencer marketing campaigns, it is important to allow influencers to share their genuine opinions about your products or services.

Remember that influencers are real people, and their followers expect them to be authentic and honest in their recommendations. Asking them to promote something they don't believe in can harm the trust relationship they have with their followers, which in turn can negatively impact your brand's perception. Instead, by allowing them to share their honest opinions, even if they are not always positive, you are building a stronger and more authentic relationship with your customers.

Furthermore, it is important to be transparent about any influencer collaborations. You should ensure that any sponsored posts or promoted content are clearly labeled as such, so consumers know it is a paid collaboration. This is not only ethical and transparent but also a legal requirement in many countries.

There are various tools and metrics that can be useful in measuring the effectiveness of influencer marketing campaigns. Here are some examples:

Engagement Rate: Measures the interaction of followers with the influencer's content. It can be calculated by dividing the number of likes and comments by the influencer's total number of followers.

Reach: Measures the exposure of the influencer's content, i.e., the number of people who have seen the content. This metric is important for assessing the visibility achieved through the collaboration.

Conversion Rate: Measures the number of people who, after seeing the influencer's content, have taken a desired action, such as making a purchase or subscribing to a service.

Cost per Acquisition (CPA): This metric measures the cost of acquiring a sale or desired action from users who have interacted with the influencer's content.

Return on Investment (ROI): Measures the profitability of the influencer collaboration, i.e., the relationship between the campaign cost and the generated revenue.

Analyzing these metrics is essential for evaluating the effectiveness of influencer marketing campaigns and making informed decisions. Some of the metrics that can be measured include post reach, engagement, website traffic generated, increase in followers, and conversions.

For example, according to a survey by Linqia, 39% of marketers plan to increase their budget for influencer marketing in the future, indicating the growing importance of this strategy in digital marketing. Furthermore, the same study found that 76% of marketers measure the success of their influencer marketing campaigns based on audience engagement and participation.

It is also important to track and measure the results of your influencer collaborations. You can use analytics tools to evaluate the effectiveness of your influencer marketing campaigns and adjust your strategies accordingly.

Chapter 12: Email Marketing: How to Build and Utilize an Effective Email List

In the world of e-commerce, building and utilizing an effective email list is crucial for maintaining a lasting and fruitful relationship with customers. Email marketing is one of the most cost-effective and efficient marketing strategies, with an average ROI of 38:1 according to a DMA Insight report. In this chapter, we will explore the necessary steps to build and utilize an effective email list that drives sales and enhances customer relationships.

Step 1: Identify Your Target Audience

The first step in building an effective email list is to identify your target audience. You need to consider who your ideal customers are and what information would be useful and relevant to them. By understanding the needs and desires of your target audience, you can create content that meets those needs and establishes a closer and more trustworthy relationship with your customers.

To build an effective email list, thorough research of your target audience is necessary. You can conduct online surveys, interviews, and analyze data from previous customers to gain a better understanding of your customers. By knowing your customers better, you can create content that is useful and relevant to them, increasing the likelihood of them subscribing to your email list.

It is also important to segment your email list based on your customers' interests and behaviors. You can segment them by their purchase history, interests and preferences, geographic location, and other relevant factors. By segmenting your list, you can create specific content for each group and increase the effectiveness of your email campaigns.

Step 2: Obtain Customer Contact Information

Once you have identified your target audience, the next step is to obtain their contact information. You can collect this information through registration forms on your website, social media giveaways or contests, or by offering exclusive discounts in exchange for contact information. It is important to request only the necessary information for your business and inform your customers how you will use their contact information.

A successful case of effective email list building is the cosmetics brand, The Body Shop. The brand focused on creating relevant and personalized content for their customers in their newsletter, including special offers and exclusive discounts for subscribers, as well as beauty tips and product updates. The Body Shop used registration forms on their website and offered discounts in exchange for contact information, allowing them to build a high-quality email list with engaged subscribers. As a result, the brand achieved a significant increase in email open rates and clicks, which in turn boosted sales and customer loyalty.

Another successful example of building an effective email list is the men's underwear brand, Mack Weldon. The brand used registration forms on their website and offered discounts in exchange for potential customers' contact information. Additionally, Mack Weldon created personalized and relevant content in their newsletter, including product recommendations and style tips. The brand also implemented an automated email strategy to send personalized emails at specific points in the customer's purchase journey, which helped increase sales and customer satisfaction.

Step 3: Utilize the Right Software

Once you have obtained your customers' contact information, it is essential to use the right software to manage your email list. There are many email marketing software options available, including Mailchimp, Constant Contact, and Campaign Monitor. These tools allow you to create and send personalized emails, automate sales funnels, measure campaign performance, and much more.

Step 4: Create Relevant and Personalized Content

Content is key to an effective email list. You need to create content that is relevant and personalized to your customers. Utilize the information you have gathered about your customers to create content that satisfies their needs and desires. Include informative and entertaining content such as blogs, videos, and tutorials, as well as special offers and exclusive discounts for your subscribers.

Step 5: Personalize Your Emails

Personalized emails have much higher open and response rates compared to generic emails. Use the information you have gathered about your customers to personalize the emails you send. Include your customers' names in the greeting, use a friendly and approachable language, and offer content and offers that are relevant to their interests. A study by Campaign Monitor found that emails with personalized content have a 29% higher open rate and a

41% higher click-through rate than generic emails. This highlights the importance of creating personalized and relevant content for your customers in your emails. For example, if your online store sells hair care products, you can create content such as styling tutorials and hair care tips that are relevant to your subscribers and help them address their needs.

In addition, including special offers and exclusive discounts for your subscribers can also be an effective way to increase engagement and sales. A report by Experian found that emails that include offers have a 48% higher transaction rate than emails without offers. Therefore, it is important to offer exclusive incentives for your subscribers and ensure they feel valued and appreciated for being part of your email list.

Step 6: Automate Sales Funnels

Automating sales funnels is an effective way to utilize an email list. You can set up a series of automated emails to be sent to your customers based on their actions, such as their website registration or product purchase. These emails can include helpful and relevant content, as well as offers and exclusive discounts to encourage sales and customer loyalty.

Step 7: Continuously Evaluate and Adjust

It is important to continuously evaluate and adjust your email list and email campaigns to improve effectiveness and conversion rates. You can use analytics tools to assess the open rates, clicks, and conversions of your emails and adjust your strategies accordingly. For example, if a certain type of email has a low open rate, you can adjust the content or subject line to improve the open rate.

Building and effectively using an email list can be a powerful marketing strategy for e-commerce. By offering exclusive discounts and promotions, valuable and personalized content, utilizing email automation, and continuously evaluating and adjusting your strategy, you can build an effective email list and increase conversion rates and customer loyalty.

Chapter 13: Social Media Marketing: How to Utilize Social Media to Boost Sales

In today's world, social media is an essential tool for e-commerce. With billions of active users worldwide, social media offers an unparalleled platform to reach new customers and promote your products and services. In this chapter, you will discover how to effectively utilize social media to boost sales and grow your online business. You will learn how to identify your target audience on social media, create engaging and relevant content, and interact with your followers to build trust and brand loyalty.

Additionally, you will learn best practices for social media posting, including when and how often to post, how to optimize your posts to maximize reach and engagement, and how to use social media advertising to reach a broader audience and increase sales. Through real-life examples of successful brands on social media, you will uncover how to create an effective social media marketing strategy and measure the success of your social media efforts. With the right tools and the right strategy, social media marketing can be a powerful tool to boost sales and grow your online business.

To effectively utilize social media in e-commerce, it is essential to identify your target audience. Social media platforms offer a wealth of demographic and behavioral information that you can use to understand your audience.

Factors such as age, gender, geographic location, interests, and online activities of your followers should be considered to create engaging and relevant content.

Once you have identified your target audience, it is important to create compelling and relevant content that captures their attention and encourages interaction. This can include posts about new products or services, special offers and promotions, informative and educational content, and entertaining content. You should also ensure to use the appropriate tone and voice for your brand and tailor your content for each social media platform.

In addition to creating engaging content, it is also important to interact with your followers on social media. Respond to their questions and comments in a timely and helpful manner, and encourage conversation and the exchange of ideas. This helps build trust and brand loyalty and establishes a closer relationship with your customers.

Another way to utilize social media to boost sales is through social media advertising. Social media platforms like Facebook, Instagram, and Twitter offer highly effective advertising tools that allow you to reach a specific audience with personalized messages and clear calls to action. By utilizing audience targeting and tracking tools, you can create highly effective advertising campaigns that drive sales and increase customer loyalty.

To make the most of social media in e-commerce, it is important to know the best practices for posting compelling and relevant content that drives sales. In terms of posting frequency, it is recommended for businesses to post regularly but avoid overwhelming their followers' feeds with too much content. The key is to find a balance that keeps followers engaged and excited about the brand without becoming overwhelming.

It is also important to optimize posts to maximize reach and engagement. This means using compelling and high-quality images and videos, using relevant hashtags to increase post visibility, and ensuring that the content is informative and entertaining. Other effective techniques include creating polls and contests to increase follower engagement and encourage interaction with the brand.

An example of an effective social media advertising campaign is Coca-Cola's "Share a Coke" campaign. In this campaign, the brand invited consumers to personalize bottle labels with their names and share photos on social media using the hashtag #shareacoke. The campaign was a great success as consumers felt personally involved and connected with the brand, and it generated a significant boost in Coca-Cola's sales.

According to a Statista report, the number of social media users worldwide is expected to reach 4.41 billion by 2025.

54% of consumers have used social media to search for products, services, and brand information, according to a GlobalWebIndex report.

A Hootsuite study revealed that 90% of marketers claim that social media has increased their businesses' visibility.

Social media advertising is a rapidly growing industry. According to an eMarketer report, social media advertising spending is expected to reach $112 billion in 2022.

A Sensis survey revealed that 79% of small businesses in Australia use social media for marketing, and 45% of businesses using social media reported an increase in sales.

These statistics demonstrate the importance and significant impact of social media marketing in today's world of e-commerce. It is crucial for any online business to have an effective social media presence to reach their target audience and generate sales.

Chapter 14: Measuring the Success of Your Online Marketing Strategy

The success of any online marketing strategy relies on the ability to measure and analyze the results. In this chapter, we will explore the different metrics you should consider to evaluate the effectiveness of your online marketing strategy and adjust your efforts accordingly.

First and foremost, it is important to establish clear and specific goals for your online marketing strategy. Do you want to increase sales, generate more website traffic, improve social media engagement, or promote a new product line? Each goal will require a different set of metrics to measure its success.

To measure the success of your e-commerce efforts, you can consider metrics such as website traffic, conversion rate, cart abandonment rate, time on site, bounce rate, and customer lifetime value. These metrics can help you assess the performance of your website, identify areas for improvement, and optimize your strategies to enhance user experience and increase sales.

For measuring the success of your social media efforts, you can consider metrics such as the number of followers, engagement (interactions), reach, conversion rate, and click-through rate. These metrics can help you evaluate the performance of your social media efforts, identify areas for improvement, and adjust your strategies to improve engagement and drive sales.

In addition to specific metrics for e-commerce and social media, you should also consider the return on investment (ROI) of your online marketing efforts. ROI allows you to evaluate the performance of your online marketing efforts in terms of investment and return. You can calculate ROI by dividing the gain obtained by the investment made in your online marketing strategy. If the ROI is positive, it means you are getting a return on your investment, indicating the success of your online marketing strategy.

There are various analytics and tracking tools you can utilize to measure and analyze the metrics of your online marketing strategy, such as Google Analytics, Facebook Insights, Hootsuite Analytics, among others. These tools enable you to evaluate your online efforts and adjust your strategy accordingly to improve performance and increase sales.

Digital advertising has become an integral part of the e-commerce world, and its impact on brands and consumers continues to grow. With digital advertising spending consistently on the rise, it is crucial for brands to measure the success of their online marketing strategies. By tracking and measuring key online marketing metrics, brands can gain a clear and objective understanding of their online advertising campaign's performance. This enables them to make informed decisions and adjust their strategies to maximize return on investment.

According to a Statista report, digital advertising spending is expected to reach $526 billion in 2024. This demonstrates the increasing importance of online advertising and the need for brands to measure and optimize their online performance. With so many online advertising options available, from social media ads to search engine advertising, it is crucial for brands to utilize key metrics to evaluate the effectiveness of their advertising campaigns.

Measuring the success of your online marketing strategy is essential for the growth and success of your online business. You must establish clear goals, identify the appropriate metrics, and utilize analytics and tracking tools to evaluate your online efforts and adjust your strategy accordingly. With an effective online marketing strategy and proper measurement of its success, you can grow your online business and achieve your sales objectives.

Chapter 15: Best Practices for Online Customer Service

Online customer service is essential for any online business seeking to retain and attract customers. In this chapter, we will explore the best practices for providing excellent online customer service, from effective communication to efficient problem resolution.

First and foremost, it is important for customers to know how to contact your company online. Provide an email address, phone number, and/or live chat option so customers can reach out to your company at any time. It is also crucial to ensure the response time is as quick as possible.

According to a study by SuperOffice, 62% of companies do not respond to customer inquiries online. However, the same study shows that response time is a significant factor in customer satisfaction, as 41% of customers expect a response within six hours. Additionally, 90% of customers are willing to wait longer for a response if they are informed about the estimated response time. These statistics highlight the importance of a fast and effective response to customer inquiries online.

Furthermore, communication should be clear and effective. Customers should feel heard and understood. It is important to respond to questions and comments in a clear and concise manner, providing necessary information in the shortest time possible. You should also ensure that the communication is friendly and empathetic, demonstrating your willingness to assist in any way necessary.

Another critical aspect of online customer service is efficiently resolving problems. Customers may encounter issues with a product or service at any time, so it is important to have a problem tracking system in place and resolve them quickly and efficiently. You should ensure that customers feel valued and that their problems are addressed seriously.

A real-world example of a company that has demonstrated excellent online customer service is Zappos, an online footwear and clothing store. The company has become renowned for its exceptional customer service and has received multiple awards for its customer-centric approach. Zappos has a dedicated team of customer service representatives available 24/7 to assist customers in resolving any issues they may have. Additionally, Zappos offers a no-questions-asked return policy for all products, making the return process quick and easy for customers. As a result, Zappos has established a reputation as a trustworthy and customer-oriented company, contributing to its success in e-commerce.

Moreover, it is important to be proactive in online customer service. Don't wait for customers to reach out to you; take the initiative to address and resolve issues before they escalate. Through regular follow-up and proactive communication, you can demonstrate to your customers that you value their business and satisfaction.

Another effective strategy for online customer service is the use of chatbots and automation. Chatbots can provide quick and effective responses to frequently asked questions, freeing up customer service agents to address more complex issues. Additionally, automation can help ensure customers receive prompt and consistent responses.

The use of chatbots and automation in online customer service is a growing trend. According to a report by Grand View Research, the global chatbot market is expected to reach $1.25 billion by 2025, driven by the need to reduce costs and improve efficiency in customer service. Furthermore, an Oracle survey revealed that 80% of companies plan to use chatbots by 2024. Automating customer service not only enhances efficiency and reduces costs but can also provide a consistent and satisfactory customer experience.

Lastly, it is important to measure customer satisfaction and regularly evaluate the effectiveness of your online customer service. Conduct regular customer satisfaction surveys to gather feedback on how you can improve your customer service. Utilize key metrics to assess the effectiveness of your online customer service and adjust your strategies accordingly.

A prime example of a company that has demonstrated excellence in online customer service is Apple. The company has implemented several strategies to ensure their customers receive the best possible customer service. Apple offers online support through live chat and email, and has a support section on their website that includes FAQs, user guides, and tutorials. Additionally, the company utilizes chatbots to provide quick and effective responses to common questions. Apple has also implemented a customer service problem tracking system that allows customers to track the status of their issues and receive real-time updates. The company regularly measures customer satisfaction through surveys and utilizes key metrics to evaluate the effectiveness of their online customer service.

Online customer service is an essential part of e-commerce and a powerful tool for customer retention and brand loyalty. By following best practices for online customer service and utilizing tools like chatbots and automation, businesses can provide efficient and high-quality customer service to their online customers.

Chapter 16: How to Maintain a Base of Loyal and Satisfied Customers

In the previous chapter, we discussed the importance of providing good online customer service to create a positive and satisfying experience for customers. In this chapter, we will delve into how to maintain a base of loyal and satisfied customers.

Maintaining customers is crucial for the long-term success of any online business. It is more cost-effective and easier to retain an existing customer than to acquire a new one. Additionally, loyal customers are more likely to recommend your business to friends and family, which can attract new customers.

One way to keep customers loyal and satisfied is by offering a loyalty program. Loyalty programs can be as simple as providing exclusive discounts to repeat customers or as complex as a reward points system. The key is to offer incentives for customers to return and make additional purchases.

A successful example of a loyalty program is Starbucks Rewards, which offers discounts, free beverages, and personalized gifts to its program members. Through this program, Starbucks has managed to maintain a base of loyal customers who return to the store to enjoy their drinks and rewards.

Another example is Amazon Prime's loyalty program, which offers free and fast shipping, access to exclusive content, and discounts on select products to its members. This program has helped Amazon maintain a base of loyal and satisfied customers who enjoy the exclusive benefits of the program.

Another way to maintain customers is by providing excellent customer service. Loyal customers feel valued and appreciated, and it is important to ensure they receive exceptional customer service. Listen to your customers' suggestions and complaints and do your best to resolve any issues. When customers feel valued, they are more likely to return to your online store.

It is also important to maintain regular communication with your customers. Email marketing is an effective tool for keeping customers informed about special offers, promotions, and other events. Additionally, email personalization can increase open and click-through rates, enhancing the likelihood of customers making repeat purchases.

The importance of maintaining regular communication with customers cannot be underestimated. According to a HubSpot study, email is one of the most effective marketing channels for customer retention and engagement. Moreover, the same study shows that email personalization can increase the open rate by 29% and the click-through rate by 41%.

Email personalization is a technique that involves using customer data to send personalized and relevant messages. According to an Accenture study, 91% of consumers are more likely to buy from brands that provide personalized offers and recommendations. This demonstrates that email personalization is an effective way to increase customer loyalty and engagement.

Furthermore, post-sale follow-up is important for maintaining loyal customers. After a customer makes a purchase, send a follow-up email to ensure they received the product and to inquire if they have any questions or concerns. This type of follow-up demonstrates that you care about the customer's experience and can help maintain their loyalty to your brand.

There are many ways to do post-sale follow-up and maintain loyal customers. One effective approach is to send personalized follow-up emails after a purchase. For example, a beauty products company could send an email thanking the customer for their purchase and offering some helpful tips for using the products. Another example is a clothing company that sends an email after the customer has received their order, asking if everything was received in good condition and if the customer is satisfied with their purchase.

It is also important to have a system in place for following up with dissatisfied customers or those who have encountered an issue with an order. If a customer has a negative experience, it is important to address the problem effectively to maintain their loyalty. For instance, an electronics company could have a 24-hour customer service hotline to resolve any issues customers may have with their products. They could also offer hassle-free returns and refunds to ensure customers are satisfied with their purchases.

Chapter 17: How to Expand Your Business Internationally - A Guide to Global E-commerce

Global e-commerce presents a unique opportunity for businesses to expand their reach and attract new customers from around the world. However, it also poses unique challenges that need to be addressed in order to succeed in the global market. In this chapter, we will explore how to expand your business internationally and overcome the obstacles of global e-commerce.

Market Research

Before expanding your business internationally, it is important to conduct thorough market research. This involves researching potential markets and determining if there is sufficient demand for your products or services in those markets. Additionally, you need to consider the logistical challenges and cultural barriers that may impact your success in international markets.

Website Localization

Your website is the gateway to your online business, and it is important to ensure that it is properly localized for the international market. This includes translating content into other languages and adapting currency, size, and brand imagery to meet the needs and preferences of local consumers. Additionally, you need to consider the legal and regulatory requirements that may vary from country to country.

International Search Engine Optimization (SEO)

To succeed in global e-commerce, it is crucial to ensure that your website is visible in local search engines. This means optimizing your website for local search engines, using relevant keywords, and tailoring your content strategy to meet the needs and preferences of local consumers.

Shipping and Logistics Considerations

Shipping and logistics can be one of the biggest challenges in global e-commerce. It is important to research local shipping options and select a reliable logistics partner that can guarantee fast and reliable delivery worldwide. You also need to consider customs requirements and local taxes that may impact shipping costs.

Global Payment Strategies

To succeed in the global market, you need to consider payment options that meet the needs and preferences of local consumers. This may include accepting different types of credit and debit cards, bank transfers, and local online payment options.

International Customer Support

Customer support is a critical aspect of global e-commerce. You need to ensure that customers from around the world can effectively communicate with your business and resolve any issues they may have. This may involve translating customer service content and hiring customer support representatives who speak multiple languages.

Analysis and Tracking of Global E-commerce Strategy Effectiveness

It is important to measure the success of your global e-commerce efforts and track key performance metrics to adjust strategies accordingly. This includes evaluating conversion rates, shopping cart abandonment rates, and customer feedback.

Additionally, you need to assess the demand for your product or service in the destination country and tailor your marketing strategy to reach your target audience in that country. This may include translating your website and marketing materials into the local language and utilizing local e-commerce platforms to reach consumers.

An effective tool for international expansion in e-commerce is the use of global e-commerce platforms such as Amazon, eBay, and Alibaba. These platforms have a global audience and can help you reach consumers worldwide. However, you need to ensure that your products or services comply with the platform's policies and meet shipping and handling requirements.

Furthermore, it is important to consider compliance with export and import regulations of the origin and destination country. These regulations may include restrictions on certain products, import taxes and tariffs, and labeling and packaging requirements.

In summary, international expansion in e-commerce can be a great opportunity to grow your business and reach new markets. However, it is important to carefully consider cultural, legal, and market factors to ensure your business succeeds overseas.

CHAPTER 18: TRENDS AND PREDICTIONS FOR THE FUTURE OF E-COMMERCE

E-commerce has experienced an unprecedented boom in recent years, and this growth is expected to continue in the future. Artificial Intelligence (AI) technology is one of the most prominent trends in e-commerce and is expected to have a significant impact on the way online sales are conducted.

Personalizing the customer experience is one area where AI is making a big difference. Businesses can use AI to collect and analyze data on customer behavior and purchasing preferences, enabling them to offer highly personalized and enhanced product recommendations in real-time. This improves the customer experience and can help increase sales.

Automating the supply chain is a key area in e-commerce, and AI is proving to be a valuable tool for optimizing processes and improving efficiency. With AI, companies can automate planning, monitoring, and control tasks in the supply chain, allowing for more effective resource management and cost reduction.

Furthermore, AI can help businesses predict product demand and inventory needs in real-time, enabling more effective inventory management. This not only reduces storage costs but also improves delivery speed by ensuring that products are available when customers need them.

Another way AI is enhancing efficiency in the supply chain is through route optimization for shipping and delivery. AI can analyze traffic data, weather conditions, and other factors to determine the fastest and most efficient shipping route, reducing delivery time and shipping costs.

Automating the supply chain can also help reduce errors in orders. With AI, companies can automate picking, packing, and shipping processes, reducing the possibility of human errors. This improves the customer experience by ensuring that orders are delivered correctly and on time.

AI is also being used to enhance online security. AI technology can help detect and prevent online fraud, improving customer security and trust in the brand. As for predictions for the future of e-commerce, AI is expected to continue transforming e-commerce and enhancing the customer experience. E-commerce is also expected to continue growing as more consumers shift to online shopping and technology continues to improve online efficiency and personalization.

Additionally, other disruptive technologies such as augmented reality (AR) and virtual reality (VR) are expected to have a significant impact on e-commerce. These technologies can enhance the customer experience by allowing them to visualize products and interact with them before making a purchase.

Augmented reality and virtual reality are technologies that have gained traction in e-commerce in recent years. These technologies have the potential to transform how customers interact with products online and significantly enhance the customer experience.

Augmented reality allows customers to overlay virtual images onto the real world, enabling them to see how a product would look in their environment. This is particularly useful for products like furniture, clothing, and accessories as it allows customers to see how a product would fit into their home or with their outfit before making a purchase. Augmented reality can also be used to provide additional information about a product, such as usage tutorials or technical data.

On the other hand, virtual reality is a technology that allows customers to experience products in a virtual environment. This is particularly useful for products that cannot be physically tested, such as travel experiences, events, or digital products. Virtual reality enables customers to virtually explore a tourist destination, attend an online event, or experience how it would be to use a digital product in a simulated environment.

In addition to improving the customer experience, augmented reality and virtual reality can also enhance efficiency in e-commerce. These technologies can help reduce costs and time associated with logistics and inventory management by allowing customers to see and experience products online before making a purchase.

Regarding predictions for the future of augmented reality and virtual reality in e-commerce, these technologies are expected to continue growing and improving in personalization and interactivity. Online retailers are expected to increasingly utilize augmented reality and virtual reality to create unique and personalized shopping experiences for customers.

As e-commerce continues to evolve, it is also important to pay attention to online privacy and security concerns. Companies must ensure compliance with regulations and protect the privacy and security of their customers online.

AI and other disruptive technologies have the potential to transform the way online sales are conducted. As e-commerce continues to grow, businesses need to be mindful of future trends and predictions to stay ahead in the industry and provide exceptional shopping experiences for their customers

.

Karlo Parker is a successful entrepreneur who has dedicated his time and effort to creating online stores for others. With extensive experience in e-commerce and a clear vision of market trends and opportunities, Karlo has helped many people make the leap into the world of e-commerce.

Since his first e-commerce project, Karlo has been dedicated to assisting people in creating online stores that are attractive, functional, and profitable. With a passion for design and technology, Karlo has created online stores for a wide variety of products and market niches, helping his clients expand their businesses and achieve their sales goals.

In addition to his e-commerce expertise, Karlo is known for his focus on customer service and satisfaction. He is always willing to listen to the needs and desires of his clients and works closely with them to ensure that their online stores meet their expectations.

In summary, Karlo Parker is a passionate and dedicated entrepreneur who has helped many people create successful online stores. With his experience in e-commerce, customer service focus, and clear understanding of market trends, Karlo is a source of knowledge and a valuable guide for anyone looking to succeed in the world of e-commerce.

r

www.ingramcontent.com/pod-product-compliance
Lightning Source LLC
Chambersburg PA
CBHW070124230526
45472CB00004B/1402